D# 206891

THE SHOP
ON HIGH STREET

The Toys and Games of
Early America

John J. Loeper

THE SHOP ON HIGH STREET

The Toys and Games of Early America

ILLUSTRATED WITH OLD PRINTS
AND WITH PHOTOGRAPHS

Atheneum   1978   New York

*The toys pictured on pages 39, 52, 57, 78 and 79 are
courtesy of the New-York Historical Society.*

Library of Congress Cataloging in Publication Data

*Loeper, John J
The shop on High Street.*

*SUMMARY: Describes toys and games available in
America during the period from 1760 to 1815.
1. Toys—United States—History—Juvenile
literature. 2. Games—United States—History—
Juvenile literature. [1. Toys. 2. Games] I. Title.
GV 1218.5.L63   688.7'2'09   77-24737
ISBN 0-689-30622-9*

*Published simultaneously in Canada by
McClelland & Stewart, Ltd.
Manufactured in the United States of America by
Halliday Lithograph Corporation
West Hanover, Massachusetts
First Edition*

To Elizabeth Apelt

Contents

TO ANY READER

As from the house your mother sees
You playing round the garden trees,
So you may see, if you will look
Through the windows of this book,
Another child, far, far away,
And in another garden, play.
But do not think you can at all,
By knocking on the window, call
That child to hear you. He intent
Is all on his play-business bent.
He does not hear; he will not look,
Nor yet be lured out of this book.
For, long ago, the truth to say,
He has grown up and gone away,
And is but a child of air
That lingers in the garden there.

A Child's Garden of Verses
by Robert Louis Stevenson
Copyright, 1905, by Charles Scribner's Sons

ONCE UPON A TIME

Once Upon a Time

History is once upon a time. It is the story of real people who once lived and worked and played. Not just famous people, but all people who lived in the past. And among these people were boys and girls who went to school, played games and loved their toys.

Once upon a time, many years ago, a doll was rocked to sleep by a little girl.

Once upon a time, in another century, a rocking horse carried a little boy to distant places only he could imagine.

Once upon a time, long since gone, toy soldiers camped on a sitting room floor.

Toys have always existed. Wherever there have been children, there have been toys. Archeology has revealed that toys are common to all ages throughout history. A modern doll can trace her ancestry back to ancient Egypt. Marbles were used by the children of primitive man, and Eskimo youngsters long ago played with toy canoes and sleds carved from walrus tusks.

This book is about the toys and games of the children of early America, in the years from 1750 to 1840. Surprisingly, they are not unlike the toys of today. But then, there is a similarity among popular toys. Certain kinds of toys can defy the barriers of time and place.

Many of the surviving toys of early America now rest on museum shelves. Like the children who owned them, the toys belong to the past. They are a part of history—a part of once upon a time. Yet they also belong to today. But once upon a time is a good beginning.

THE SHOP
ON HIGH STREET

The Shop on High Street

A heavy wagon drawn by two stout horses rumbled over the cobblestones of old Philadelphia. It was delivering merchandise unloaded from ships at the docks to shopkeepers in the city.

One large wooden chest resting on top of barrels and crates was addressed to: MR. LORING—HIGH STREET AT SECOND.

As the wagon clattered along through the crowded streets, children, noticing the wooden chest, pointed with excitement. A shipment was on its way to Mr. Loring. What new wonders did the chest hold?

In 1791, Philadelphia was the capital of the United States and the greatest city in America. It had a booming economy and was the cultural center of the new country. Many of the citizens were men and women of wealth and learning. One writer of the time commented, "No other city is so rich, so fashionable, so extravagant!"

The city was an excitement of shops, taverns and amusements. It boasted an amphitheater where a circus offered, "Surprising Feats on the Tight Rope," and "A Great Variety of Equestrian Exercises." And its theaters offered the latest plays from London.

7

On High Street, the main thoroughfare of the city, was the High Street Market, famous throughout the states. Here farmers set up stalls in long, open buildings to sell their produce. On market days the place overflowed with customers.

Surrounding the Marketplace were rows of shops displaying merchandise from around the world. Stores of every description offered "quality goods" and "exceptional items" for ladies and gentlemen.

But to the children of Philadelphia, the most exciting shop on High Street belonged to Mr. Loring. His shop offered "amusements for little masters and mistresses." Mr. Loring's shop was a wonderland of toys. Most of the toy shops in early America were located in the large cities. Boston had a flourishing toy shop by 1745, and a New York shop advertised in 1770 "An arrival of Dutch and English toys." In one of his letters, Benjamin Franklin related, "When I was a child of seven, my friends filled my little pocket with halfpence. I went directly to a shop where they sold toys for children . . ."

In the country, rural ingenuity produced homespun toys. Whittling was almost a national pastime and whistles and trinkets were carved out of native woods. Poor roads prevented toymakers from bringing their wares to the smaller communities. It was the city children who enjoyed the marvels created by master toymakers.

There was a time in America, in city and country, when buying a toy might have been considered frivolous. But as the country prospered, buying toys became more common. Toy shops offered a variety of merchandise from inexpensive paper cutouts to expensive mechanical wonders.

All of Mr. Loring's stock came from Europe where the best toys were made. Craftsmen in Germany and Holland had been manufacturing toys since the sixteenth century. There were toymakers guilds in the Middle Ages. English and French dolls were known the world over, and the making of dollhouses for privileged children was common in eighteenth century Europe.

In England, such famous woodworkers as Thomas Sheraton and Thomas Chippendale furnished dollhouses with exquisite miniatures of their furniture. Mr. Loring's had such a dollhouse, a replica of an English Georgian mansion. It had paneled rooms, and the brass chandeliers in its tiny chambers held real wax candles. There was a parlor with upholstered chairs; a dining room with a table set with china and crystal and a master bedroom with a canopied bed. The little girls of Philadelphia dreamed of owning such a magnificent doll house.

The boys were more interested in the parade of toy soldiers. The Johann Hilgert family of Nuremburg, Germany, supplied Mr. Loring with forty different models of Prussian soldiers. They were made of tin or pewter, and their uniforms were hand-painted. There were also wooden cannons and castles to house the soldiers.

One shelf in Mr. Loring's shop held a zoo of wooden animals. There was a Noah's ark brimming with pairs of animal passengers and an orchestra of carved bears playing various musical instruments. There were cows, lambs,

goats, dogs and horses. And there was a bronze duck made in France able to "drink, eat, quack and splash about."

Everything needed for a well-ordered farm was available at Mr. Loring's—tiny wagons, ploughs, hoes, forks and shovels. A playroom pasture could be stocked with a shepherd and his sheep, hens and ducks with real feathers and fat, rosy pigs. A toymaker's apprentice in Germany was expected to carve "a galloping horse, well-proportioned and finely painted to look natural" as a test of skill. The carved animals were beautifully executed.

Then there were the wooden nutcrackers. These are traditionally German, dating back to the sixteenth century. Grim looking wooden soldiers, monks and servants, each had a movable lower jaw. A nut placed in the figure's mouth could be cracked by the action of a wooden lever. They were known as "German gobblers."

Another shelf held music boxes and toy instruments. There were miniature regimental drums and bright brass bugles. Mr. Loring took particular pride in his collection of "pipes, fiddles, rattles and drums." Still another shelf held a collection of dolls. Dolls were made of wood, kid leather or wax. Many had movable arms and legs. The faces were usually painted on, but a few had glass eyes. Brown was the favorite color for doll's eyes until Queen Victoria's accession to the British throne in 1837. Her eye coloring made blue-eyed dolls fashionable.

The most elegant of Mr. Loring's collection wore a blue satin dress with a full skirt and had an elaborate wig of human hair. Her locks were gathered into a loop on top of her head, held there with pink ribbons. The simplest dolls were small wooden ones carved by German peasants. These tiny, inexpensive creatures were called penny-woodens.

But the most fascinating and exotic doll ever housed in the High Street shop was delivered to Mr. Loring in the wooden chest. When the chest arrived, he opened it carefully and removed the straw packing. Inside was a doll made in Paris. It had been ordered by a wealthy Philadelphian for his daughter's birthday. This special gift was a mechanical doll who danced, twirled and bowed. She was displayed in Mr. Loring's window for several days to the delight of passing children. Girls pressed their noses against the shop windows to watch the miraculous "living doll." Boys were bewitched by her graceful movements. Mechanical dolls, powered by wind-up springs, were not unusual in the eighteenth century. Three of the most extraordinary mechanical dolls were made in France around 1780. One could sketch a portrait of Queen Marie Antoinette. Another could write a letter in perfect penmanship. The third, a lady seated at a harmonium (a kind of organ), played a melody. Her head turned from side to side as her fingers glided over the keyboard. And, her performance finished, she stood up and bowed!

One day, a distinguished resident of Philadelphia visited Mr. Loring's shop. Mrs. Washington, wife of President Washington, stopped by to examine his toys. At the time, Mr. Loring was entertaining some young customers with his wares. A boy was working a puppet on strings; a girl was arranging tiny cast iron pots and pans in a toy kitchen; and a little boy was riding a brightly painted rocking horse. Mrs. Washington watched for a while and was amused by their enjoyment. Then she selected a pull toy, a wooden donkey on wheels, as a gift for a young cousin in Virginia. It had been carved by a craftsman in Berchtesgaden, Germany. Mr. Loring assured the First Lady that his toys were "the best available in all our fifteen states!"

The inventory of Mr. Loring's stock was impressive. Among other things it listed: a stag on wheels, a fine horse with saddle and rider, pecking chickens on a board, children's chairs, figures that could be pulled along or jumped, a moving clown, all kinds of elegant coaches with four, six or eight horses, pop guns, boats, cradles with or with-

out baby, cricket cages, tiny butter churns and sleds of all sizes.

Not everyone agreed that children should have such interesting toys. Toward the end of the eighteenth century some people in America began to speak out about the "money wasted" on toys and children. One writer said dolls, rocking horses and toy animals were "useless pleasures." Another suggested that all any child needed for amusement was a pencil and paper. "A child's time out of school must be filled with some duty," one expert preached. Cutting potatoes, watering horses, picking berries, spooling yarn or feeding swine."

But the allure of toys was too strong. Despite the protests and complaints, dolls, lead soldiers and toy animals had captured America's children, as they had captured children everywhere. Toy shops, like Mr. Loring's on High Street, spread and multiplied. As the country grew and transportation improved, toys invaded the outposts. About 1850, America would develop a toy industry of its own. Toys were here to stay.

A CHEST OF TOYS

About Adam Barkley's Toy Army

"General" Adam Barkley placed his brass spy glass to one eye and searched for the enemy. Surrounding him was an army of valiant soldiers.

It was a winter afternoon in 1795, and the battlefield was the plank floor of the Barkley dining room in Baltimore. Stationed at one end of the room were fifty foot soldiers of stamped tin. Behind them were twenty-five cavalrymen, wooden carriages and toy cannons.

Across the room stood wooden soldiers with white belts and plumed hats. Scattered among them were British guards wearing bearskin caps, red-trousered hussars and mounted guards on white horses. In the center of the room stood a wooden fortress armed with tiny cannons. Colorful banners flew from the turrets, and the drawbridge was secured for battle.

The General surveyed the room and decided he needed reinforcements. From a wooden box he enlisted twenty additional tin figures. They wore the uniforms of the

Prussian army of "Old Fritz," Frederick the Great. He mustered eight wooden knights from another box, and pressed a brightly uniformed officer into service.

Toy soldiers are as old as childhood. In ancient times Egyptian children and then Roman children played with clay figures. During the Middle Ages and later in the Renaissance of the fifteenth and sixteenth centuries, skilled workers made toy soldiers out of gold and silver for the children of the wealthy. War games using toy soldiers were an important part of the education of every young prince. In 1760, Monseigneur le Dauphin, heir to the throne of France, received a present of a toy army with thirty detachments of infantry and thirty squadrons of cavalry.

"War games are for boys from 12 years of age to 150," wrote one authority. "And for that more intelligent sort of girl who likes boys' games and books."

The eighteenth century was a time of special interest

in the toy soldier. All the toy centers of the world produced them. Germany, especially, supplied children with miniature armies and military gear of every description.

Tin soldiers started their triumphant march to the world at large from the German city of Nuremberg. Production there dates back to 1578. They were flat, painted figures made of various metallic alloys. Ordinary tin soldiers were cheap and sold by the dozen. More carefully made models were expensive.

Wooden soldiers were also of German origin. They were carved and hand-painted by craftsmen. Many had movable parts. Some figures could salute, others had jointed arms and legs for marching.

Following the Revolutionary War, American generals and soldiers began to appear in toy shops. But the traditional toy soldier was the European warrior dressed in the uniform of his native land.

Available, also, were boxes of tin or wooden figures called "battle packs." A printed description of some famous battle was included along with the soldiers, guns, trees and houses necessary to stage the toy combat.

General Barkley did not own any battle packs. His army was a mixture of sizes, shapes and nationalities. Adam did not plan on a military career when he grew up. Yet the fascination of a toy army did cast its spell.

He readied his fortress for battle and moved his toy horsemen closer to the front.

Once again he searched the room with his brass spy glass. He sighted the enemy!

There it was, crouched under a chair in a far corner of the room. Tabby, the cat, stretched and yawned as she awoke from an afternoon nap.

"Prepare for battle!" Adam commanded.

His toy soldiers stood ready.

"The enemy approaches!" Adam called out.

With that, Tabby strolled across the battlefield, knocking down tin soldiers and toppling toy cannons. With a sweep of her tail she captured the fort.

The casualties were high. Adam realized that his army needed more drill and discipline. Tabby walked out of the room unaware of the destruction she had caused. As Adam packed his toys for another day, the enemy reappeared. She rubbed herself against the General's leg, purring with victory.

The Chinese Chariot

The box was there when Peter came downstairs for breakfast. It sat on the hall table and was the most curious box he had ever seen. It was bright orange, oval, and had a hinged lid. On its sides were designs of unusual flowers and figures. He suspected that the box belonged to his father, undoubtedly a souvenir of his recent journey to China.

During the early 1800s, American ships wandered over the world in the India trade. Peter's father, a merchant seaman, sailed aboard the *Royal Dragon* each time it left New York bound for some exotic port.

When Peter reached the kitchen he sat down at the breakfast table by the fireplace. He addressed his father.

"Good morning, sir!"

"Good morning, Peter," his father answered.

"Good morning, Mother!"

"Good morning, Peter," his mother added. She set a bowl of heated milk on the table.

As Peter sipped the warm milk, his father spoke. "When I was in Canton, I visited a native bazaar. Here they sold everything—silks, fruits and vegetables, articles of brass and copper. One merchant had brightly painted boxes of various sizes and shapes. I asked what they were, and he opened one to show me. When I looked inside, I decided that my son should have one. So, I purchased a box, and it is yours. It is on the hall table."

Peter's eyes brightened. The box was his! "Oh, thank you, Father!" he said. "May I get it and look inside?"

"When you finish breakfast," his mother ordered.

His meal completed, Peter rushed to the box. Slowly he raised the lid. Inside was a toy chariot drawn by two plumed horses. It was made of lacquered wood and gaily painted. The small wheels turned on wooden axles and the black horses raised their front legs in captured motion. A wooden driver wearing a square hat stood in the chariot holding reins of silken cord.

Until 1840, traders were allowed access to only one Chinese port, Canton. The Emperor of China would not open other ports to foreigners. Yet people in Europe and America were so eager to buy spices and other rare products from China that Canton became a busy port. Everyday ships from around the world sailed in and out of its harbor.

Toys and miniatures had been made in China for centuries. Chinese artisans delighted in intricate and delicate work. Many of their toys and miniatures were carried to the New World by trading ships. American children like Peter were enchanted by strange playthings from a faraway land.

All that day Peter played with his new toy. At one time

the chariot carried a Persian prince on a dangerous mission. At another time, it brought back captured treasure from a distant city. It transported a Chinese king in search of a kidnapped princess, and it fought in imaginary battles against hoards of enemy troops.

That night Peter placed the chariot on a table next to his bed. In his dreams he relived the adventures of the day. He felt the rush of air against his face as the two plumed horses galloped along. He crossed strange landscapes as the Chinese chariot carried him through dreamland.

The chariot was his toy for many years and remained a treasured souvenior of a faraway land.

Hugh Lambert's Little Theater

Some children of Charleston, South Carolina, gathered around Hugh Lambert's little theater. The young producer stood behind the tiny stage ready to lift the curtain on the first act of "David and Goliath." He was also the playwright. He had written the script using his father's Bible.

The two assistants, his younger brother and sister, nervously held the puppet-actors by their strings. They hoped the show would be a success. Handwritten playbills had been distributed among the audience assuring them that this "new and surprising feat of dramatics" performed on June 12, 1798 in the Lambert sitting room, would entertain and amuse them.

By 1798 theater was accepted by most Americans. This had not always been the case. Quaker opposition to "profane stage shows" kept theater illegitimate in Philadelphia until 1789. Religious groups in other sections opposed the theater, calling it "immoral" and the "devil's work." In those days, Hugh's little theater would have been considered an improper toy. Now, however, Charleston had a theater as did New York and Philadelphia. Audiences enjoyed plays by Shakespeare and London hits like *The*

Beggar's Opera, and thought it acceptable and proper.

Hugh's little theater was constructed of gilded wood and had velvet curtains that could be raised or lowered. The rear of the stage was fitted with slots where backdrops of scenery could be easily fitted. The theater, manufactured in England, came with four changes of scenery, one for each season of the year. "David and Goliath," taking certain liberties with the biblical account, would be staged in winter.

Toy theaters and puppets are old toys. They have been enjoyed by children throughout history. One of the earliest

forms of play theater is the glove or finger puppet. The cloth figures fit the hand like a glove and are manipulated by the fingers.

Hand puppets had their roots in antiquity. They were used in the Middle Ages to dramatize stories from the Bible; such shows were given at fairs and in the streets. Puppet shows in England were known as "motions" and their operators as "motion men." The most familiar names in puppetry are Punch and Judy. These characters evolved over many centuries. Punch was first referred to as Punchinello. Punch and Judy were the first European puppets to perform in America. They gave a performance in Philadelphia on December 30, 1742.

Shadow figures were another form of toy theater. Flat figures were cut out of cardboard and attached to holding rods. The manipulator held the figures in front of a backdrop and moved them about. Shadow shows were popular in colonial America.

In Europe, toy theaters were a standard item for toymakers. Some of them reproduced famous opera houses and theaters to scale. One of the most famous toy theaters belonged to a German prince. It was a complete miniature of an actual theater. Joseph Haydn, the composer, wrote operas for it, and the German poet, Goethe, helped in making scenery for its Lilliputian productions. It was Goethe who wrote that "children must have plays and puppets."

Also available in toy shops were paper theaters. These were much less expensive. Stage sets and figures were printed on paper sheets. These could be cut out and mounted on wood or cardboard. One toymaker offered paper theaters "a penny plain; twopence if colored." Some picture sheets also copied real theaters. Current operas and plays were available for home presentation complete with script and stage directions.

A certain German toymaker offered paper theaters "for all kinds of fantasies about knights and fairies, all brilliantly colored and drawn to exact proportion."

As early as 1790, American toy shops offered puppets and marionettes. One toy catalogue of 1800 listed a theater with "ten movable characters, all neatly dressed and painted."

At last the moment arrived. The audience waited in hushed anticipation as the little curtain lifted. Goliath, the

Philistine giant, stood at center stage and threatened in a gruff voice, "Let the armies of Israel choose a man to fight with me!" The audience heckled the Old Testament villain. David appeared with his slingshot. The audience cheered. "This day will I deliver my people from the enemy!" he shouted out. The audience cheered again. Being familiar with the biblical story, they knew what the outcome would be—David would slay Goliath with a stone. Hugh knew that his show was a success. He smiled with delight as the action on stage continued.

Next week he would present another production. Using the same puppets in different dress, he planned to present Moses at the Red Sea.

His sister would sew the costumes, and his brother would play the role of an Egyptian general.

"But I want to be Moses!" his brother protested.

"I let you play David while I played Goliath," Hugh answered. "Now it is my turn to play the hero!"

His brother was not happy. Hugh decided to cheer him up. He did not want to lose an assistant.

"We will do a play about General Washington, and you can be the General," Hugh promised.

His brother was pleased. It would be an honor to play the role of America's greatest hero.

About King Nutcracker

Late on Christmas Eve of 1801, nine year old Anton Weber gathered with his brothers and sisters in the parlor of their Pennsylvania home. They sang a Christmas hymn as their father and mother lighted the tiny candles clipped onto the branches of a fir tree.

The tree, decorated with candy and nuts and toys, soon sparkled with flickering candlelight. Beneath the tree was a toy landscape inhabited by dolls and toy animals. One woolly sheep stood on three legs, a victim of Christmas past.

And on a nearby table a solemn King Nutcracker guarded mounds of nuts and Christmas cookies.

Anton loved the stern-faced King Nutcracker. Every Christmas for as long as he could remember, King Nutcracker was taken from his storage box to rule the holiday season.

The Germans, after the British, were the second largest European group to settle in America. Between 1727 and 1776, more than sixty-eight thousand Germans came through the port of Philadelphia. Following the Revolution, a new wave of German immigrants arrived. The

Germans brought with them their culture and folk traditions. During festive times in Germany, toys played a major role. Carved storks bearing wooden babies were given as wedding presents, and at shooting festivals (Schutzenfeste), the targets were elaborately carved animals or creatures from folk tales. One famous target had a goblin that popped out of a chimney when the bull's eye was hit.

The German celebration of Christmas has always been associated with toys. They were used as decorations on the Christmas tree; and Christmas gardens were assembled beneath the tree, where children might set up their toys. The Weber's garden had a village of tiny houses. A bridge crossed a pond made from a fragment of mirror. It led to a forest of pine branches where toy animals hid among the needles. A hill of moss held grazing sheep including the three-legged one. And in a cave of rocks a Nativity scene was arranged on a bed of straw. The figures of Mary, Joseph and the shepherds gathered around the sleeping baby. Elaborate Christmas gardens were an important part of a German Christmas.

The Moravians, a German religious sect, constructed a *putz* at Christmas time. The Moravians established two major settlements in America, one in Bethlehem, Pennsylvania, and the other in Salem, North Carolina. In both communities, the building of the Christmas *putz* was an annual tradition. *Putz* comes from the German word, *putzen*, meaning "to decorate." It is a miniature portrayal of the Nativity with landscaping, tiny trees,

gnarled stumps and rocks. A typical *putz* might contain hundreds of objects and figures. The stable with the holy family was always the central subject. Every Moravian home had its *putz*. Some occupied an entire room and took weeks to build. Many of the figures were carved by toy-makers in Germany and brought to America by the Moravian settlers.

After lighting the tree, Anton and his family sat down for coffee and cake. Standing at the center of the table was a Christmas pyramid. Its candles were lighted causing it to revolve slowly. A procession of wooden angels went round and round on tiered platforms.

The Christmas pyramid was a holiday innovation. Frames for holding candles were built from three or four wooden rods. These formed the shape of a pyramid. The pyramid was once a substitute for the Christmas tree.

For a time, partly as a conservation measure, German rulers forbade the cutting down of fir trees for indoor use at Christmas time. There were severe penalties for any violation of these decrees. The ingenuity of the toymaker devised a substitute. He constructed a wooden frame in the shape of a fir tree. As time passed, these pyramids became more and more elaborate. Eventually, wooden fans or turbines were fixed at the top. Turned by the heat of the burning candles, the fan caused inner platforms to revolve. On the platforms were carved angels, animals, soldiers or religious figures in procession.

Following refreshments, the Weber family exchanged simple presents. Anton received a pruneman as a gift.

Dolls and figures made of dried prunes and raisins were made for the holiday season. These prunemen had prune faces, prune limbs and wore clothing with raisin buttons. A popular pruneman was the figure of the chimneysweep. He was thought to bring good luck to his owner.

But prunemen were often short-lived. Prunes and raisins were meant to be eaten!

Presents exchanged, Anton's mother announced that the children were free to nibble cookies and nuts. They raced to the table where King Nutcracker guarded the Christmas treats. These wooden figures, usually soldiers, were used to crack nuts. The hard shell was placed in the creature's mouth. A lever clamped his jaws together and

crushed the shell. King Nutcracker always occupied a prominent place. He was extolled in song and story. A Christmas without the Nutcracker was no Christmas at all. The composer Tchaikovsky made him an enchanted prince in his *Nutcracker Suite.*

More Christmas songs were sung as the candles on the tree burned lower. The mound of cookies and nuts diminished. Soon it was time for bed.

Anton climbed the stairs hugging his pruneman. It had been a wonderful Christmas Eve. The tree, the garden and King Nutcracker had made this an enchanted evening.

Tomorrow, Christmas Day, the family would travel the snow-covered roads in a horse-drawn sleigh to visit Grandmother Weber. There, a dinner of roast goose awaited them and Grandmother's own King Nutcracker, a relic of her childhood in Germany, would preside over the Christmas feast.

Samuel and His Noah's Ark

Young Samuel Gwynn sat on a bench in the Congregational Church of Newport, Rhode Island listening to a preacher relate the Bible story of Noah and the Ark.

It was a rainy Sunday in October of 1802. The drumming sound of the rain on the church roof made the tale from Genesis more realistic. The pious voice of the preacher droned on:

"God saw that the wickedness of man was great and it grieved his heart. And the Lord said, "I will destroy man, whom I have created, from the face of the earth, man and beast and creeping things and birds of the air, for I regret that I have made them."

But one man, Noah, was just and guiltless and found favor in the eyes of the Lord. God said to Noah, "I am going to destroy all living creatures, for the earth is filled with violence. Therefore build an ark of wood and seal it inside and out with pitch." Then the Lord instructed Noah to make the ark 450 feet long, 75 feet wide and 45 feet high. A window was to be built for the ark; a door was to be set in one side; and the ark was to have three stories. Then the Lord commanded Noah to bring two of every living creature into the ark. Noah did all that the Lord commanded. Two by two all living things went with Noah into the ark.

And torrents of rain fell upon the earth and flooded it. But Noah, his family and the living creatures were safely sheltered and protected in the ark.

The great flood lasted for 150 days. Then the rain stopped and eventually the waters subsided. When the earth was dry again, God spoke to Noah saying, "Go forth from the ark with the living things so that they may breed abundantly upon the earth." Thus a fresh new start was given to the earth and God promised never to destroy the earth again by water. To seal his promise he caused a rainbow to appear in the sky."

As the preacher spoke, Samuel imagined his own toy ark filled with its animal passengers afloat on the waters of the flood. The story of Noah is captivating. The notion of bringing pairs of living creatures aboard a large boat has a certain appeal, especially for young people. Toymakers, recognizing this, have produced toy arks for hundreds of years. They are available today in toy shops. One of the earliest toy arks was made in Germany in the sixteenth century. This ark held eighty-four carved wooden animals, including a pair of dragons!

The usual toy ark is a small boat holding a rectangular house. Often the roof is hinged or detachable, so the animals can be easily put in or taken out of the house.

The size, number of animals included, and decoration may vary. Some toy arks might have an exotic menagerie —hippos, camels, giraffes and elephants. Others might include domestic animals—horses, cows, sheep and goats. One ark might be gaily painted while another might be of plain, undecorated wood. Most of the toy arks in early America were imported from Europe. The few made here were carved by folk artists.

In early days, many parents considered the toy ark an educational toy. It allowed a child to play yet taught a Bible story. It was one of the few toys allowed on Sunday.

Many communities in early America practiced a strict observance of Sunday. There were even fines imposed for Sabbath-breaking. Everyone, including children, was expected to attend church and spend the day in a solemn manner. A story is told of a New England boy and his father, walking to church one Sunday morning. The boy pointed out a squirrel frolicking in the trees, and the father twisted the boy's ear with the warning that "squirrels are neither seen nor mentioned on the Sabbath!"

To play with a toy on the Sabbath was forbidden. Yet the ark was allowed. Parents claimed that it was not play but Bible study. For this reason the ark was called a "Lord's Day Toy."

A long, dull sermon followed the biblical reading. Samuel feigned attention but in his mind he was on the ark with Noah. He was in charge of the animals. As the ark bobbed along over the waters of the flood, Samuel carried hay to the sheep and calmed nervous lions and leopards. He cleaned and checked cages and stalls, reporting to Noah that everything was under control.

A stern nudge from his father brought him back to reality. The service was over.

Leaving the church with his parents, he found that the rain had stopped.

"Just a lull in the storm," his father remarked looking at the grey sky. "It will rain again this afternoon."

"May I stay by the fire and play with my ark?" Samuel asked. His mother looked at her husband.

"Yes, Samuel," his father said. "Then you will learn well the story of Noah and how God cares for all his creatures."

That afternoon Samuel returned to the ark. His toy took on the dimension of a real vessel, and the little animals came alive. And better than being just a helper, Samuel decided that he would be Noah. He steered the ark across the kitchen floor, around dangerous table legs and through chairs. A wooden pig fell overboard and had to be rescued. One of the lions tried to escape. It was a dangerous voyage, but by late afternoon, the imaginary flood waters had subsided and the ark was put away for another Sunday.

A Journey Through Europe

The orange light of the setting sun spilled into the sitting room of the Spencer home in Williamsburg, Virginia. It illuminated the portrait of Thomas Jefferson hanging above the mantle and tinted the far wall. The President, inaugurated in March of 1801, was a personal friend of Mr. Spencer and had just negotiated the purchase of the Louisiana Territory from Napoleon of France. This made the game of a Journey Through Europe more interesting.

The children huddled around the game, spread out on the carpeted floor.

"Look!" shouted little Amy Spencer to her brothers and sisters. "I have arrived in Paris!"

The children had heard their parents speak of France and Mr. Jefferson's efforts.

"Perhaps Napoleon will invite you to tea," her brother joked.

The children laughed.

It was fun to move through the great cities of Europe printed on the game board. Players moved along a marked route according to the throw of their dice.

43

Board games like this were as common in the eighteenth century as they are today. Most of them were educational and attempted to teach facts of history and geography. A Trip Around the Globe, Landmarks of World History and Walker's Geographical Pastime were among the host of available games. The first board game was invented in England about 1759, and it spawned a multitude of similar games.

"I take five moves!" Amy exclaimed as she threw the dice and they shoved her marker along. "Soon I will cross the channel and visit London!"

Playing cards were also used as instructional devices. Printers decorated cards with "educational" words and

pictures. They were intended to instruct children as they
played. Bits of knowledge covered everything from history and arithmetic to astronomy, music, logic and even
Latin. One early pack was intended to teach girls the various cuts of meat.

Before printing presses were used in America, early
settlers fashioned playing cards from leaves, bark or deerskin. Following the introduction of printing, many estab-

Juft like the Kite the giddy Youth
Soars upon pleafure's wing,
Forgeting, that fome fkilful guide,
Should regulate the ftring.

The Rocking Horfe perfues its courfe
Directed by your hand
Children fhould thus their friends obey
And do what they command.

The Whiptop to the froward Child
This lefson doth impart,
The fcourge muſt quickly be apply'd
To bend the ftubborn Heart.

The freighted Ship from diftant Port
Return'd to Britain's fhore,
The Merchant's induftry's repaid
His anxious fears are o'er.

lishments took to producing playing cards. Benjamin Franklin was a leading manufacturer of his time.

Before the Revolution, cards bore pictures of English royalty. The king of hearts showed George III. After the war, decks carried pictures of Americans. George Washington appeared on the King of Hearts, and military heroes on others. Some decks featured American Indians with feathered chiefs on the lead cards.

Certain religious groups cautioned that playing cards were "the devil's picture book." But card games persisted. While adults played Whist and Cribbage, the children played simpler games like Snipsnapsnorum. This game required players to call out "Snip," "Snap," "Snorum" when they played certain cards.

In 1762, a young English printer invented a unique teaching tool. He cut up a map into small pieces for the teaching of geography. The pieces had to be put back together in their proper places to form a completed map. This was the start of the jigsaw puzzle. By 1770 the jigsaw puzzle was commonplace. All sorts of jigsaw puzzles were manufactured. Some taught lessons, but most were just for fun.

Mrs. Spencer entered the room.

"Come, children," she said. "We will have to light candles if you continue with your game."

"But I have not reached London," Amy pleaded.

"No, but you have nearly reached bedtime," Mrs. Spencer answered. Reluctantly, A Journey Through Europe was put away for another time.

A WORLD OF DOLLS

Abigail Allen's Doll Collection

Nine-year-old Abigail Allen sat in her upstairs playroom in the city of Boston surrounded by her dolls. She was composing a letter to her uncle.

Dearest Uncle Roger,

    I wish to thank you for the beautiful doll you brought from Spain. She is truly the loveliest doll in my collection. Mother claims that she might be the Queen of Spain, she is so richly dressed and decorated. Father tells me that those are real pearls sewn onto her costume and that her tiny earrings are of real gold.

    How good you are to me and how much I shall miss you! I pray that your next voyage will be a safe one and that you will return very soon.

Your devoted niece,
Abigail

Signing her name, Abigail folded and sealed the letter. She would give it to her father who would see to it that the letter was delivered to her Uncle Roger. He was a sea captain, and his ship was setting sail for the West Indies. It was this uncle who had brought Abigail most of her dolls. Each time he visited a foreign port, he purchased a doll for his niece.

Some of the dolls were old and rare. Abigail owned a doll from ancient Rome. It was a carved ivory image that had found its way from antiquity to a street vendor's stall. She also owned a clay doll from Mexico that had once belonged to an Aztec child.

Abigail's English and French dolls were the most beautiful. Their bodies were made of wood with peg-jointed arms and legs. The faces had sharp little wooden noses and bright red cheeks. Some had painted hair, while others had ringlets of real hair. Most had glass eyes and all were elaborately dressed. The eighteenth century was an age of elegance. Dolls were made to look like grown-up ladies rather than children. And they were not always toys.

That very morning a Boston newspaper had advertised, "At Mrs. Hannah Teats, a dressmaker on Summer Street, is to be seen a doll in the latest fashion recently brought from London by Captain White." Dolls were not only toys but ambassadors of fashion. They carried the news of the latest styles from Paris and London to ladies in other lands. In 1751 an English magazine noted that, "several dolls with different dresses have been sent to the Czarina of Russia to show her the manner of dressing at present among English ladies of fashion."

Abigail's most beautiful dolls were really fashion dolls, dressed in magnificent materials. They wore silks, velvets, laces and embroidery. French and English dressmakers created splendid outfits for such dolls, and hairdressers manufactured fine wigs. Even the dolls' accessories were elaborate. No fashion doll was complete without a wardrobe of hats, slippers, gloves, jewelry and mother-of-pearl fans.

Not all of Abigail's dolls were ladies, however. She had gentlemen in her collection as well. There was an Oxford don in cap and gown, and a French prince wearing a plumed hat. She also had a Franciscan monk in hooded robe and leather sandals.

Another interesting doll in Abigail's collection was a pedlar doll. These dolls represented the old ladies who roamed the English countryside selling pots, pans and other household necessities. Called "Notion Nannies," the pedlar dolls were popular in the eighteenth century. In contrast with the fashion dolls, the Notion Nannies wore simple dresses over which they held out their trays containing a selection of miniature merchandise. Abigail's pedlar doll wore a full white apron and carried a basket of knickknacks. Among her wares were tiny spools of thread, wool, knitting needles, sealing wax and quills.

Abigail was fortunate in owning a doll from Japan. For more than two centuries Japan had been closed to the Western world. No foreigners, except for a few Dutch traders, were permitted to go to Japan. Japanese traders were likewise forbidden to leave the country. As a result,

Japanese products were scarce. Abigail's uncle had purchased the doll from a Dutch sailor who brought it from
Nagasaki.

Dolls are an important part of Japanese culture. There
are two doll festivals in the Japanese calendar. One, on
March 3, is the girls' doll festival, and the boys' doll festival is held on May 5. On these occasions ceremonial dolls
are displayed. The boys' dolls represent ancient heroes and
warriors. The girls' dolls wear the costumes of the ancient
Japanese court.

Abigail's Japanese doll wore a bright blue kimono, a
loose robe with wide sleeves and a broad sash. Her body
was made of stuffed silk and she had real hair. Her delicate
features were painted on her silken face. Abigail named
her Hana which means "flower" in Japanese.

Still another curiosity in Abigail's collection was the figure of an angel in flowing robes, playing a golden harp.
It had come from the city of Naples in Italy and had been
part of a Nativity scene.

As early as 1478 the churches and citizens of Naples
had displayed elaborate Nativity scenes, with figures from
the Christmas story. Mary, Joseph, shepherds, kings and
angels were portrayed by dressed dolls. In some convents,
nuns spent the entire year dressing the dolls for the Christmas display. People vied with each other in the splendor of
their Christmas figures. It was said that some of the Christmas dolls rivaled kings and queens in the richness of their
clothing.

Abigail's angel was of carved wood with a painted face. She wore a flowing robe of pink velvet tied at the waist with a gold cord. Her harp was made of wood and had strings that could be plucked.

The newest addition to Abigail's collection had been purchased by her uncle in Malaga on the Mediterranean coast of Spain, in the area called Andalusia. This section of Spain is known for its bright clothing.

The doll's head was made of wax and had come from either Germany or Italy. German and Italian toymakers had been producing wax dolls since 1650.

Wax was poured into a clay mould to form a lifelike head. The head was then attached to a cloth or wooden body and hair was added to complete the picture. The texture and color of the wax gave the appearance of flesh. Many of the dolls were exported and dressed at their destination.

Abigail's Spanish doll was outfitted in the tiered gown of an Andalusian lady. Her skirt had many rows of ruffled silk and she wore a black lace mantilla, supported by a comb. Along the neckline of her dress, tiny pearls had been sewn to form a rich border. Her wax ears held hoops of gold.

Among all the elegant and rare dolls in Abigail's playroom, there was a special one. It was a simple rag doll stuffed and sewn by hand. Her arm was tattered and her face stained. She seemed out of place among the others. But a rag doll can be hugged and taken off to bed.

At the end of the day when the playroom door was closed, the wax face of the Spanish lady turned envious and the glass eyes of the fashion dolls glared with jealousy. They were left behind on the shelf while the rag doll was chosen to stay with her mistress.

About Rebecca Rooker's "Play-Prettie"

I have a dolly made of corn;
The other made of fruit.
Dolly wears a cornshuck gown;
My apple man, a suit.

In a sunny kitchen in Lyme, Connecticut, eight-year-old Rebecca Rooker sat by the fire making a "play-prettie." It was November of 1780. She had sewn some scraps of cloth into a human form and was stuffing it with straw. She pushed and plumped the straw until the doll was shaped and firm.

For centuries, rag dolls have been loved by little girls. At first the daughters of the colonists made dolls of deerskin, since cloth was valuable. They stuffed these with dried grass, pine needles or milkweed floss. Features were painted or drawn on, and a few tufts of wool were glued on for hair. As cloth became more plentiful, the dolls' bodies became calico. Yarn was used for hair and buttons for eyes. Sometimes rag dolls were given apple heads.

A peeled apple was placed in the sun to dry. As its moisture evaporated the fruit began to shrivel. As it shriveled, it could be molded. By careful pinching, a nose, a chin, a cheek could be formed. Daily the desired features were pinched and pressed into shape until the apple was completely dry. Then the apple head was placed on a stick and inserted into the stuffed body of the doll. Apple dolls have interesting faces. As time passes, the heads become leathery and take on a rich brown color.

Corn also produced toys for colonial children. Boys dueled with cornstalk swords and used slices of corncob as wheels for toy wagons. The girls made cornhusk dolls. By tying husks in certain ways, they could create legless dolls with wide skirts.

A bundle of husks was dampened and folded together at the middle. A head was formed by tying the bundle near the folded top. A slim roll of husk was inserted to form arms and a second tie formed a waist. The bottom was fluffed and trimmed to form the skirt. Often cornsilk hair was glued on as a final touch.

As time passed, the cornhusk dolls became more sophisticated. Clever girls added more detail. The dolls wore cornhusk bonnets, aprons and kerchiefs. Some carried cornhusk parasols.

Whittled clothes-pegs, used to hold laundry on the clothesline, often disappeared from a mother's basket. Girls used them to make little armless dolls. With a painted face and a full skirt, the clothes-peg doll made a pretty plaything.

The ingenuity of colonial girls transformed many common materials into dolls. Twigs, spools, seashells and wooden spoons became little creatures when they were painted and dressed.

Rebecca finished stuffing her rag doll. It needed a dress and a bonnet, but she would make those tomorrow. In the meantime, she drew on the doll's face. Taking a piece of charred wood from the fireplace, she drew crude eyes, a nose and a mouth. She giggled when she saw the finished product. "I shall call her Bonnie!" she exclaimed. "She will have a pretty name, if not a pretty face!"

Over the years, Bonnie's features wore away and her seams had to be restitched several times. Once the family dog chewed on her arm, and Rebecca watched while her mother repaired the damage. The guilty hound crawled under a table to repent.

Every night the doll shared Rebecca's bed, and she was the silent companion of the daylight hours. She listened attentively to Rebecca's secrets and soaked her tears after a scolding. Bonnie was more than a "play-prettie." She became a loyal and trusted friend.

Paper Dolls

At the time of the American Revolution, the ability to cut patterns from paper was considered a useful accomplishment for young ladies. Betsy Ross is said to have created a five-pointed star for the first American flag with a snip of her scissors.

A fundamental cutting exercise was to fashion a string of paper people. A long strip of paper folded accordion style was cut in the shape of half a figure and unfolded. A whole row of little figures holding hands was the pleasant result.

Cutting silhouettes or shadowgraphs was equally popular. Profiles of the face or figure were cut from black paper and pasted on white. Young girls enjoyed testing their skill by capturing a good likeness. Nelly Custis cut out profiles of her grandparents, George and Martha Washington, while living at Mount Vernon.

Yet, despite the ability of American girls to cut paper figures, the idea of a cutout doll originated in England.

In 1791 an advertisement appeared in an American newspaper:

A new and pretty invention has been lately received from London. It is a toy for little girls, but is so pleasing that grown women will also want to play with it. The doll is a young female figure cut out of stout cardboard about eight inches high. It has simply curled hair and is dressed in underclothing. With it go eight complete sets of dresses which are to be cut out of paper.

This heralded the birth of the paper doll.

Originally called "English dolls," the paper dolls were copied by printers in other countries. At first, they were

expensive, but as printing techniques improved, the price of paper dolls dropped. Soon they were available for just a few pennies.

In some instances paper dolls were part of an elaborate setting. One set printed in 1802 showed an entertainment at the Royal Palace in Hanover. The walls of the ballroom were of colored and gilded cardboard. Paper figures in fancy dress gathered around a pianist playing a paper piano. Another set of the period simulated an outdoor cafe with paper diners, waiters and tiny tables. One spectacular set had paper dolls worshiping in a cardboard cathedral. Complete with altars and printed stained glass windows, this particular set included eighty-six pieces.

Once introduced, paper dolls never lost their popularity. They were a common amusement found in the toy chests of early America.

About Beth Dean's
Tiny Kitchen

—Eight-year-old Beth Deane patted a crust of mud in a tiny tin pie dish. She filled it with sand and decorated the top with small pebbles. Then she placed it in the oven to bake.

Her kitchen was small but amply furnished. It had three walls and measured eighteen inches long, nine inches deep and twelve inches high. At the center of the rear wall stood a fireplace with an oven built into the side of the chimney. Shelves along the two side walls were crowded with miniature utensils. There were pewter plates and saucepans of copper all properly tinned. There were crockery mixing bowls and iron pots. There were pitchers and baskets and a handled tureen.

On the floor of the toy room stood a kettle, a butter churn, a spinning wheel, a three legged stool and a long handled iron skillet. And suspended from the mantel were ladles, mixing spoons and a tin lantern.

Beth's kitchen also stored a dolls' dinner service in decorated porcelain. It provided four settings of plates and cups with saucers. She also had tiny knives, forks and spoons made of pewter. Her newest treasure, imported from France, was a lovely china tea pot.

Toy kitchens were not uncommon. The kitchen was the heart of the early American home. Here the mother prepared meals, the children played on rainy days and the family gathered to talk. It was only natural that children would want a toy version of a favorite room. Tinsmiths, potters, weavers and ironmongers all created smaller versions of their wares for young housekeepers, and indulgent fathers constructed the miniature rooms out of scrap lumber. A fine example of a toy kitchen may be seen in the Metropolitan Museum of Art in New York City. It was made about 1790.

German toymakers offered the "Nuremberg Kitchen." This was a large box open on one side. The interior held an exact model of a sixteenth century south German kitchen.

A few toy kitchens were manufactured in this country. Around 1790 tin makers in Maine and Connecticut were making toy tinware for children including little toy kitchens. In 1784, a Mr. Boyle announced in a New York newspaper, "doll dishes, plates and platters of pewter." One manufacturer boasted tiny copper kettles "ready to boil water in" and stewpots "fit for broth."

Kitchens were also a part of most dollhouses. One English dollhouse assembled in the eighteenth century has a basement kitchen crammed with over one hundred pots, pans, bowls and dishes.

For those children who wanted to provide for toy kitchens, European toymakers offered miniature butcher shops and bakery shops. A young merchant could offer customers carved and painted cuts of wooden meat or wooden cakes and tarts.

But, Beth, like most children, depended on her own imagination and ingenuity. While her pie "baked," she mixed a batch of clay muffins and prepared a stone roast for the oven. Tomorrow she planned a party. Her friends would join her and bring their dolls. "Tea" would be served in the porcelain cups, and the dolls would enjoy the bounty of Beth Deane's toy kitchen.

Martha Reading's Mansion

The doll house was not big like the old German ones, huge affairs standing five or six feet tall. Nor was it elaborate like the fine English ones, some actually set on a cabinet base with carved legs. This doll house was a homemade one. Yet it had a quaint charm unmatched by the finest of professional houses. It was not too large. It could stand on a table or rest comfortably in a corner of the playroom. Outside it was painted a rust red with white trim around the windows and doorway.

"It's the most beautiful house I have ever seen!" little Martha Reading exclaimed that Christmas morning of 1805.

"Your father built it, and your brother and I furnished it," her mother told her.

The doll house was patterned after their own home in Wethersfield, Connecticut. Of course it had been modified somewhat, considering that dolls need less space than humans. Two steps led to the front door. The door was made of paneled pine with a tiny brass knocker. On the top step was fixed a small boot scraper.

"Mr. Butler made these for me at his forge," her father

explained. "He also made the tiny candlesticks and the kitchen pots and pans."

There was a center hall with a polished staircase. To the left was a sitting room. It had a braided rag rug, a pair of pine benches and four spindle chairs. In the center of the room stood a pedestal table holding a miniature candlestick. The windows were hung with homespun and pictures were pasted on the whitewashed walls. To the right was the kitchen. It had a big fireplace surrounded by saucepans and a footed kettle. There were basins no bigger than thimbles and a plank table set with pottery dishes. Upstairs were a bedroom and a nursery.

The bedroom held a canopied bed with a fluffy feather

mattress, a tall chest of drawers, a horsehide trunk and an armchair. The nursery was furnished with a low bed, a hooded cradle, a round table and a rocking chair.

"Your brother carved and fashioned the furniture," her mother told Martha.

"And your mother braided the rugs and sewed the curtains," her father added.

"It is a mansion!" Martha marveled.

That afternoon Martha's dolls moved into their new quarters. It was quite comfortable, and the penny-wooden dolls enjoyed the feather bed. After life in a discarded hat-box, they agreed with Martha that this new house was indeed a mansion!

Dollhouses have a long history. There is evidence to show that Egyptian children, and later, little Greeks and Romans, played with dollhouses. Some of the most famous dollhouses were made in Europe. In 1557, the Duke of Bavaria commissioned the building of a dollhouse for his little daughter. It was four stories high with a total of seventeen doors and sixty-three windows. The lower floor held a stable, a cow barn, a wine cellar and a coach house. On the second floor was the kitchen. The third floor had a ballroom and bedchambers. On the top floor there were workrooms, nurseries and a chapel complete with a miniature priest and choirboys.

Some Dutch dollhouses of the sixteenth century had carved chairs upholstered in fine tapestry and beds dressed with tiny linen sheets. In England and America, toy deal-

ers advertised, "German and Dutch Baby Houses with All Sorts of Furniture."

The earliest existing dollhouse of early America was built in Boston around 1744. It is made of wood and is two stories high. It has two open rooms in the front and two open rooms at the back, the center partition acting as rear wall for each room. The rooms have built-in fireplaces with accompanying shelves.

A fine American dollhouse was built by a New York minister, the Reverend Dr. Philip Brett, in 1838. This toy residence boasts a library with a collection of miniature books. It holds a postage-stamp-sized edition of Robert Burns' Poems and a tiny Bible printed in 1780.

Another beautiful dollhouse was constructed and furnished by a Philadelphia cabinetmaker named Voegler. Its rooms are decorated with hand-painted wallpaper, needlework carpets, miniature oil paintings and magnificently carved and veneered furniture.

Martha's dollhouse was not a miniature mansion. It did not compare with finer houses made by toymakers and cabinetmakers. It was a simple house.

Yet, dollhouses, like real houses, do not depend on size and furnishings to make them loved.

OUTDOOR FUN

A Pocketful of Marbles

Benjamin Benton plunged his hand into the pocket of his leather breeches and pulled out a handful of marbles.

"I'll show you my best one," he said to the other boys. He knelt and poured the marbles onto the ground. His playmates joined him. Sorting through the marbles, he picked out a large translucent green sphere streaked with red lines.

"Here it is!" he exclaimed. "My uncle brought it to me from England. "It's agate."

"What's agate?" one of the boys asked.

"It's a kind of stone and it comes in different colors," Benjamin answered.

"Is it a good shooter?" another boy asked.

Benjamin responded by flicking the marble across the hard ground. "See!" he answered proudly.

* * *

The game of marbles is one of the oldest of all games. It may even have been played by cavemen. Many smooth round pebbles have been found along with other relics of prehistoric times. It was a common game in ancient Egypt and was played in Greece and Rome. It was well known, too, in the Middle Ages.

In early America, the game of marbles was played much as it is today. A ring was drawn on any hard flat surface with marbles placed inside the ring. Each player then tried to knock marbles out of the ring with a shooter marble, sometimes called a knuckler.

To "knuckle down at taws" was a phrase used by colonial boys about to play a game of marbles. Taw was another name for the shooter marble.

> *Knuckle down to your Taw,*
> *Aim well, shoot away.*
> *Keep out of the Ring,*
> *You'll soon learn to Play.*

These lines are found in *A Pretty Little Pocketbook*, a children's book published in 1771.

The game of marbles has many variations, and marbles are propelled in various ways. In some games they are rolled or thrown; in others they are shot by flicking them from the thumb and finger.

In plunkers, a marble is rolled along for an opponent to aim at. In pots, marbles are aimed at small holes dug in the ground. But ring taw or ringers as it is known today is the most popular game played with marbles.

Marbles themselves vary in size and composition. The larger ones are used as shooters and the smaller ones as nibs, or target marbles. In 1805 a New York toy shop offered:

Our Special 5 Cent Bag—made of strong calico with a draw string, containing 1 large shooter, 10 common gray marbles, 2 imitation agates and 2 glass marbles.

Boys who did not own manufactured marbles had to devise substitutes. Musketballs made good shooters and, on

farms, a game of marbles could be played with nuts, cranberries or crabapples.

Benjamin traced a circle in the dirt with his finger. "Let's have a game," he said.

The other boys gathered round.

Part of the game of ring taw is called "capturing." As marbles are shot out of the ring they may be "captured" or taken by the successful shooter.

"I'll even put my agate in the ring," Benjamin announced with confidence. The others cheered.

Before long, Benjamin saw his precious marble fly out of the circle, expelled by his best friend's knuckler. "Are you going to capture it?" he asked anxiously. The other boys cried out, "Yes, take it! It's yours!"

His friend pondered the question. "No," he said, handing it over. "It's your best marble, and I am your best friend."

Benjamin smiled. He was happy to keep both friend and marble.

Jackknives

In July of 1800, young Moses Mounts wrote in his diary, "Today I received a fine knife with a bone handle. I shall carve a spoon for mother and some amusement for myself."

While the city children had things from toy shops, country children had to settle for cruder playthings. Rag dolls, sewn and stuffed by indulgent mothers and grandmothers, were the treasures of country girls. And toys carved out of native woods provided pleasure for boys.

Wood was abundant in early America. Contemporary accounts speak of a landscape "overspread with trees" and "overgrown with woods." Wood was available for every purpose. It was used to build log houses and it was used to heat them. It was used to produce utensils and tools. It supplied furniture and it supplied children with toys.

A boy's jackknife was a prized possession. Many a farm lad worked long and hard to earn enough money to buy a good knife. A country boy's stock of toys was largely supplied by his own jackknife. The yellow birch trees of New England; the hardwood forests of the central states and the pine trees of the South provided the raw material needed to create whistles, windmills and whimsical figures.

The word "jack" was used to refer to a boy. A jack was someone simple and unrefined. Words like "jack-in-the-box" and "jack-o-lantern" reflect this. Hence, a jack-knife was a boy's knife—a simple tool.

With this simple tool boys carved whistles out of willow branches and figures out of boards. Many of the animal and human figures were amusing interpretations of nature. They were out of proportion and strangely colored. A boy carved and decorated his toys according to his artistic ability. One horse might be as small as a dog. Another might be painted green. An unsteady hand with a paint brush might produce a cockeyed cow or a spotted mouse.

Motion toys were carved by more skillful boys. One of these was the hamppelman. He was a delightful jumping man whose popularity swept across early America. Some adults feared that exposure to the toy's gyrations might

cause birth defects in the unborn. Yet, despite this grave concern, the hamppleman continued to jump. He was a flat human figure with hinged arms and legs. These were attached to a cord which, when pulled, caused his limbs to move up and down.

Other motion toys were whirligigs, dancing men and pecking birds. Whirligigs are any toys with a whirling or turning feature. A typical whirligig might be a soldier whose arms spun around or a bird whose wings circled. Often whirligigs were used as weathervanes as well as toys. In Washington Irving's *Legend of Sleepy Hollow* a reference is made to a whirligig or wind toy.

Thus, while the busy dame bustled about the house, . . . honest Balt did sit smoking his evening pipe, watching the achievements of a little wooden warrior, who, armed with a sword in each hand, was most valiantly fighting the wind on the pinnacle of the barn.

The dancing man was a carved figure with hinged feet. He was attached to a wooden rod and could be made to dance by tapping the rod. A boy with a good sense of rhythm could tap his dancing man to any tune.

The pecking bird is an ancient folk toy. It dates back almost 1500 years and is still made today in some European countries. It consists of a wooden bird mounted on a paddle. The head and tail of the bird are hinged to the body with wooden pegs or nails. When the paddle is moved in an up-and-down fashion, the bird pecks at the board and bobs its tail.

During the 1790s French missionaries brought a curious toy back from China. The French children called it an "emigrette"—a little immigrant. Its popularity spread across France and soon crossed the Atlantic. Children in America called it yo-yo. Yo-yos were easily carved by clever whittlers. Strangely enough, the yo-yo went out of fashion and did not reappear in the United States until the 1920s.

A thoughtful boy might use his knife to carve out a doll for his sister or a ladle for his mother's kitchen. ". . . . the New England boy's whittling is his alphabet" observed Daniel Webster, the American statesman. With his jackknife a boy found amusement while he learned valuable skills. He discovered how to put things together with pegs or with nails.

He learned to know wood. He knew which wood took a high polish; which woods were pliable and which were stiff. He developed skill in searching the forest to find the wood fitted to his purpose. The right curve in a sapling might be whittled into a runner for a sled. A gnarled root might hold the beginning of a toy horse. Elder or sumac were the best woods for whistles.

The country toys may have lacked the sophistication of those produced by professional toymakers. Yet, they served their purpose as well as any fine plaything.

How Jonathan Moore's Kite
Inspired Dr. Franklin

It was a windy afternoon in March of 1752. Twelve-year-old Jonathon Moore walked along the streets of Philadelphia headed toward an open field at the city's edge. He carried with him a kite made of wood and oiled cloth. He had made it according to directions found in an old volume from his father's bookshelf.

> You must take a piece of Linnen Cloth and cut into a proper shape. Take two light sticks and crosse the same. Fasten the cloth to the sticks and smeare all over with Linseed Oyle. Tie a length of small rope and rayse it in the wind.

Kites are thousands of years old. They originated in China and were brought to Europe by explorers who went to the Far East. Sailors delighted in returning home with gay colored Chinese kites for their children. And European children took up kite flying with enthusiasm.

When the new world was colonized, kites were brought to America. They provided a pleasant pastime for colonial children. Benjamin Franklin wrote of a time when, as a boy, he tied his kite to a stick. Then he lay on his back in a pond and held onto the stick. He tells us that he was "drawn along the surface of the water in a very agreeable manner . . . and with the greatest pleasure imaginable."

This very day Mr. Franklin happened to pass Jonathon on the street.

Mr. Franklin stopped. "Where are you going, young man?" he asked.

"To Hart's Field to fly my kite, sir," Jonathon answered.

"I have been fascinated by kites since boyhood," said Franklin. "May I accompany you? I am weary of work and need a little play."

"Of course, sir," replied Jonathon politely.

The two walked along while Mr. Franklin discussed air currents and theories of flight. Jonathon understood little but pretended interest. "The bird's bone is hollow. Lightness is essential."

Jonathon nodded.

"Now, with kites, cedar is the best wood," Mr. Franklin continued. "And I prefer a large, thin silk handkerchief. Tie the corners of the handkerchief to the extremities of crossed wood and be certain to add a tail."

When the pair reached the open field, Franklin helped Jonathon send the kite aloft. It rose into the sky as they fed it more and more rope. Jonathon could feel the tug of the kite in the wind and thought that it might lift him with it.

"Excellent, my boy!" Mr. Franklin exclaimed. "The kite is ten times higher than any building in the city!"

Suddenly a bright smile crossed his face. "That's it, my boy! A kite is the very thing I need!"

Jonathon looked puzzled.

"You see, my lad, I have been doing some experimentation with electricity. I contend that lightning is an electrical charge in the sky and that it can be attracted by a metallic object. My problem is to get a piece of metal high enough to attract the lightning. I thought of a building but there are none sufficiently tall. But a kite! I never thought of a kite! A kite with a piece of metal attached! Of course!"

In June of 1752, Mr. Franklin, with the help of his son,

flew a kite during a thunderstorm. He describes the experiment in his own words:

> To the top of the upright stick of the kite is to be fixed
> a sharp pointed wire, rising a foot or more above the
> wood. To the end of the twine, next to the hand, is to
> be tied a silk ribbon, and where the twine and silk join,
> a key may be fastened. . . . As soon as thunder clouds
> come over the kite, the pointed wire will draw the elec-
> tric fire from them, and the kite, with all the twine, will
> be electrified. . . . And when the rain has wetted the
> kite and twine, so that it can conduct the electric fire
> freely, you will find it stream out plentifully from the
> key . . .

Franklin collected the "electric fire," in a Leyden jar, a glass tube devised by Dutch scientists to store electricity.

When news of Franklin's experiment reached Europe, it brought him fame as a scientist. He had proved that lightning was electricity. The King of France gave him an award, and he was elected to various honor societies in Europe.

An immediate result of his experiment was the invention of the lightning rod to protect buildings.

When Jonathon heard of Mr. Franklin's experiment, he remembered that day at Hart's Field. He was pleased that his toy had helped inspire a famous gentleman.

A Horse Named Lightning

Faster and faster he rode. Up and down. Up and down. "Faster, Lightning!" he shouted. The little horse responded to the command.

His mother, observing the wild ride from the kitchen door, called out. "Hiram! Slow down!"

Gradually he brought his horse to a halt and climbed off. He stroked the animal's muzzle. "Good boy, Lightning," he whispered.

Hiram's rocking horse had been a birthday present. It was a fine animal, made of wood and with a mane of golden flax. Painted a rich chestnut brown, Lightning stood on rockers of bent wood.

* * *

Wooden horses date back to ancient times. According to legend, the Greeks entered Troy in a wooden horse. Unable to take the city by force, they built a hollow wooden horse and him some soldiers inside. When it sat alone at the gates of the city, the Trojans thought the horse was a present. So they took it into Troy. That night, under cover of darkness, the Greeks climbed out of the horse and unlocked the city gates. The Greek army entered and captured the city.

Some army posts, as late as 1860, used wooden horses as punishment. A soldier might be sentenced to sit on the horse for some neglect of duty. There he would endure the taunts of his comrades. It was a military dunce stool.

Down through the years, toy horses of all sizes and shapes have been manufactured. The hobby horse, for example, was a popular plaything. It is a horse head made of wood or some other material placed on a stick. Straddling the stick, the rider pretended to canter, trot or gallop. The hobby horse is mentioned in Mother Goose:

> *I had a little hobby horse*
> *And it was dapple gray,*
> *Its head was made of pea-straw,*
> *Its tail was made of hay.*

Just who put a horse on rockers is not known but it was a clever innovation. It gave a toy horse motion.

Rockers or "bends" had been used on cradles since the Middle Ages. About 1765 it is said that Benjamin Franklin applied "bends" to a chair and invented the rocking chair. This, no doubt, inspired some toymaker to make a rocking horse.

The earliest rocking horses date back to the late eighteenth century. In 1785, a William Long advertised in the *Pennsylvania Packet* that he specialized in making "rocking horses of all sizes." And in 1800, a Mr. C. Swift was billed twenty-seven dollars by the Philadelphia toy firm of John and William Wigglesworth for "one middle size rocking horse." The receipted bill is among other manuscripts in a museum collection.

Early rocking horses have the upper body of the horse mounted on oversized rockers. On the body there was a wooden seat or saddle for the rider. Later rocking horses show the full body of the horse with the legs attached to narrow rockers. They are more realistic, many displaying manes, tails, harness and stirrups.

As with other things, the rocking horse changed over the years. Toy makers added more detail and improved the design. Some toymakers even covered the body with horsehide and used glass eyes for ultimate realism.

After resting for a few minutes, Hiram again mounted his steed.

"Giddap, Lightning!" he ordered.

The little horse began to rock. Up and down; back and forth.

The two were off on an imaginary journey that would take them to faraway places. They traveled through exotic lands in pursuit of fictious criminals or searched for some missing princess.

Back and forth; up and down.

Back and forth; up and down.

Jed Ashley's "Rubber" Ball

Jed Ashley lived on the Ohio frontier. There were no "store-boughten" toys here. A boy growing up in the woods had to amuse himself. He observed the wild animals and played with the family dog. He whittled with his Barlow knife and practiced throwing a tomahawk. He climbed trees and skipped pebbles over the surface of a pond.

Jed's one "toy" was a present from a friendly Lenape Indian. It was a bouncing ball. The ball was not made of rubber. Rubber was not in use until after 1839. Jed's ball had been made by wrapping thin strips of bark smeared with the sap and gum from trees. Properly wrapped, the ball bounced.

Bouncing balls were a novelty. The balls used in early America were usually made of wood, cork or stuffed leather. And they were solid and heavy.

Jed had few playmates. Distances between farms were great and made frequent visiting impossible. His "rubber" ball provided amusement for long, lonesome hours. He taught the family dog to catch the ball as it bounced.

He learned to keep it in motion by continually hitting it with his hand. He devised trick throws.

Once, when a young cousin from the East visited the farm, Jed entertained him with his amazing "bouncing" ball.

"It's magic!" his cousin exclaimed.

"Yep!" Jed answered. "Indian magic!"

The Marching Band

Joshua Clark's marching band assembled early on the morning of July 4, 1802. They met at the town square of their New England village.

It was Joshua's idea to gather his friends for a holiday parade. Each owned a toy musical instrument. One brought a toy hunting horn; another a toy cornet. There were five toy bugles and seven toy drums. Joshua brought his toy fox horn.

The marchers lined up and received final instructions from their leader. The "music" began and off they went through the village.

"Children like to make noise. They would rather make a sound than listen to one," claimed an eighteenth century child expert. Rattles and noisemakers have been enjoyed by children for centuries. Children in early America banged on their mother's pots and pans and were frequently reminded that "children should be seen, not heard!"

Babies were given rattles to amuse themselves. The early colonists fashioned baby rattles from gourds. By the time of the American Revolution, rattles were being crafted by silversmiths like Paul Revere. Babies made noise with their rattles; their older brothers and sisters created sound with other noisemakers. In 1775, a Philadelphia merchant offered children "Toy drums made from empty nail kegs making a loud noise."

The German-made "wasserpfeife" or water whistle, was a popular noisemaker. Filled with water, the whistle imitated the warbling of birds. Tin horns were available in toy shops, as were cymbals, wooden clackers and jingling bells.

Moving from noise to "music," a toy piano was offered in Boston by 1820 and other toy instruments were available on special order. Toy violins, harps and flutes were produced for youthful "musicians." The sounds produced by such instruments were uniformly bad.

"Stop that racket!" a voice shouted from an upstairs window.

"What is that awful noise?" another voice called out.

"Can't a person sleep?" a third voice yelled.

The sleeping villagers had been awakened by Joshua's

marching band. Yet despite the complaints, the band played on.

"See!" Joshua said, pointing to the heads popping out of bedroom windows. "They like us! Let's march around one more time!"

In Sun and Snow

It was said that Ford's Hill provided the best sledding in Vermont. It had just the right slope, was free of trees and was a short walk from town. Climbing to its crest, boys and girls boarded their sleds for the long, fast ride downhill. In New Jersey, Larson's Pond claimed the best skating in winter and swimming in summer. The water that cooled the heat of July froze to a smooth, free surface in wintertime.

During the cold winters, on frozen lakes and ponds, children went ice skating on "Holland scates" and "Brass scates in different sizes." Down snow-covered hills and slopes, children rode sleds with wooden runners. With the arrival of warmer weather, ball playing, hop-scotch, tag and blindman's buff took over. As it is today, it was then. The children of early America moved through the year with seasonal activities.

Boys played football much of the year. Less structured than today's sport, it was described as "a leather bag kicked about from one to the other." Others called it a "bloody and wicked business" resulting in "bruises, scrapes and broken bones."

Shuttlecock was played by all. With paddles called battledores, the shuttlecock, a feathered cork ball, was bounced from player to player.

The ball is struck with Art and Care
and drove impetuous through the Air.

Younger children played singing games. "Here We Go Round the Mulberry Bush"; "Ring Around a Rosey"; "Quaker, How Art Thee?" and "London Bridge Is Falling Down" were popular. Voices sang out the same verses used today. If it were possible, a modern child could journey back to join a circle of "Ring Around a Rosey" and find the same words and motions.

Ford's Hill, Larson's Pond and other favorite ponds, hills and meadows across the early American landscape provided outdoor recreation for active boys and girls.

Crandall's HEAVY ARTILLERY.

MECHANICAL
AND
TECHNICAL TOYS

Mechanical and Technical Toys

"What fun!" exclaimed the Bradley twins as they watched the two wooden monkeys dance and lift their hats.

"Wind it again, father!" they pleaded.

Their father obliged and once again the two monkeys twirled on their wooden box. They spun round and round, lifting their hats and waving their tails.

Their father had purchased the toy for his daughters' birthday. "The shop had one with a mule kicking his hind legs and another with a bear balancing a ball. But I wanted the two monkeys." Mr. Bradley laughed. "One monkey for each of you!"

Strangely enough, mechanical toys have been around since 1000 A.D. During the Middle Ages these "magic" toys were used during festivals for religious purposes. Figures of the virgin and the saints were made to move their limbs or close their eyes by a flow of sand over a wooden power wheel. As the sand ran over the paddle wheel, it caused gears to turn and create animation.

Interest in mechanical toys, however, reached its height in the eighteenth century. The use of clockworks, the motion of wheels and gears powered by the gradual release of tension in a coiled spring, brought mechanical toys to a peak of perfection.

The young Louis XIV, King of France, owned performing toy soldiers made of sterling silver. Each figure held a clockwork mechanism. An extensive collection of mechanical toys was owned by Marie Antoinette, the Queen of France, and was described at length in the *National Encyclopedia*.

The toy factories of Germany, especially those in Nuremberg, became a center for the manufacture of mechanical wonders. The list of automated toys seemed endless: a dog chasing a rabbit, a soldier playing a fiddle, a dancing doll, a kicking mule, a flying angel and every variety of moving thing. French toymakers also constructed elaborate mechanical toys. Using clockworks, a large performing horse was geared to complete several stunts.

These mechanical toys were exported to America and sold in toy shops. Although some may have reached nurseries and play rooms, more sat in parlors for the amusement of adults.

Other intriguing toys were created using lenses and mirrors. By 1650, the secret of the "magic lantern" was known. It was the predecessor of our modern slide projector and the basic principle the same. Figures painted or drawn on glass were projected onto a white surface using a lens and a lamp. A 1720 dictionary defined the magic lantern as "an optical device enabling one to see spectres in the dark upon a white wall."

In 1818, an English scientist invented the kaleidoscope. This simple toy is made by placing three mirrors together

to form a hollow triangle. Any object resting on one surface is reflected by the other two, forming a symmetrical pattern. Bits of colored glass or sand enclosed in a mirror tube can be rotated to produce an endless variety of patterns.

About 1830, another technical device, called a zoetrope, appeared in the toy shops of England, France and America. A row of figures was drawn on a long strip of paper attached to the inside wall of a revolving cylinder. Some part of each figure, an arm or a leg, appeared in a slightly different position in each new picture. When the cylinder was rotated, the figures blended into one figure in motion. The zoetrope was a crude form of optical animation, a motion picture. It may not have featured a Mickey Mouse or Donald Duck, but it did offer such "startling actions" as "a deer bounding," "a bull charging," and "a horse leaping over a hurdle."

Although not thought of as toys, children received spying glasses, magnifying lenses, scales and prisms as playthings. Many pleasant hours were passed watching a prism break sunlight into a spectrum of bright colors or examining a leaf or insect under a magnifying glass.

But for the moment, the dancing monkeys fascinated the Bradley twins. Nothing was more wonderful than their new toy. They wound it over and over again to make the monkeys dance.

Finally, their father intervened. "The monkeys will drop over from exhaustion!" he joked. "You had better give them a rest!"

TOYS TO VISIT

Toys to Visit

The doll is old
Her dress is torn;
The toy horse lost its tail;
A guard without his helmet;
A boat without a sail.

The toys are old;
From other days,
Both time and playing show,
Yet they were loved
And treasured once
By children, long ago.

But children grow
And toys do not,
For Playland sets no ends,
And dooms the toys to wondering,
"Where are my little friends?"

Many state, local and private museums own collections of
old toys. Examples of the toys described in this book as

well as other antique playthings may be visited at the following places:

THE PERELMAN ANTIQUE TOY MUSEUM
  in Philadelphia, Pennsylvania

THE SMITHSONIAN INSTITUTION
  in Washington, D.C.

THE ABBY ALDRICH ROCKEFELLER
FOLK ART COLLECTION
  at Williamsburg, Virginia

THE MUSEUM OF YESTERDAY'S TOYS
  in St. Augustine, Florida

THE MUSEUM OF THE CITY OF NEW YORK
  in New York City

THE VAN CORTLAND MUSEUM
  in New York City

THE MUSEUM OF OLD DOLLS AND TOYS
  in Brattleboro, Vermont

YESTERDAY'S MUSEUM
  in Sandwich, Massachusetts

THE CHILDREN'S MUSEUM
  in Boston, Massachusetts

THE HENRY FORD MUSEUM
  at Dearborn, Michigan

THE SMITH TOY COLLECTION
  at Crown Center, Kansas City, Missouri

THE MUSEUM OF SCIENCE AND INDUSTRY
  in Chicago, Illinois

THE CLEVELAND MUSEUM OF ART
  in Cleveland, Ohio

THE PHOENIX ART MUSEUM
   in Phoenix, Arizona

KNOTT'S BERRY FARM
   in Buena Park, California

MUSEUM OF HISTORY AND INDUSTRY
   in Seattle, Washington

CLIFF HOUSE
   in San Francisco, California

BIBLIOGRAPHY

Bibliography

CHRISTOPHER, CATHERINE. *Complete Book of Doll Making and Collecting*. Greystone Press, New York, 1949.

DESMONDE, KAY. *Dolls*. Octopus Books, London, 1974.

BISHOP, ROBERT. *American Folk Sculpture*. E.P. Dutton & Co., New York, 1974.

EARLE, ALICE M. *Child Life In Colonial Days*. Macmillan, New York, 1927.

FRASER, ANTONIA. *Dolls*. G. P. Putnam's Sons, New York, 1967.

FREEMAN, G. L. & R. S. *Yesterday's Toys*. Century House, Watkins Glen, New York, 1962.

FRITZSCH, KARL & BACHMAN, MANFRED. *An Illustrated History of Toys*. English text by Ruth Michaelis & Patrick Murray. Abbey Library, London, 1932.

HOLME, GEOFFREY. *Children's Toys of Yesterday*. London, 1932.

JACOBS, F. J. *A History of Dollhouses*. Scribner's Sons, New York, 1965.

LAUSANNE, EDITA. *The Golden Age of Toys*. English text by D. B. Tubbs. New York, Graphic Society, 1965.

METCALF, HARLAN. *Whittlin' Whistles and Thingamajigs*. Stackpole Books, Harrisburg, 1974.

OSTROW, ALBERT. *The Complete Card Player*. Grosset & Dunlap, New York, 1945.

PETTIT, FLORENCE H. *Whirligigs and Whimmy Diddles.* Thomas Y. Crowell, New York, 1972.

PLUMB, J. H. "The Commercialization of Childhood." *Horizon.* Vol. XVIII No. 4. American Heritage Publishing, New York, 1976.

WHITE, GWEN. *A Book of Dolls.* Macmillan, New York, 1956.